WITHDRAWN

Frank Thomas

SPORTS REPORTS

Frank Thomas

Star First Baseman

Dean Spiros

Enslow Publishers, Inc.

44 Fadem Road   PO Box 38
Box 699   Aldershot
Springfield, NJ 07081   Hants GU12 6BP
USA   UK

Library of Congress Cataloging-in-Publication Data

Spiros, Dean.
   Frank Thomas : star first baseman / Dean Spiros.
      p. cm. – (Sports reports)
   Includes bibliographical references and index.
   Summary: Profiles the personal life and sports career of the superstar first
baseman for the Chicago White Sox baseball team.
      ISBN 0-89490-659-3
      1. Thomas, Frank, 1968– —Juvenile literature. 2. Baseball players—United
States—Biography—Juvenile literature. [1. Thomas, Frank, 1968– . 2. Baseball
players. 3. Afro-Americans—Biography] I. Title. II. Series.
GV865. T45S65 1996
796.357′092—dc20
[B]   95-38496
                                                                                    CIP
                                                                                     AC

Printed in the United States of America

10 9 8 7 6 5 4 3 2

Photo Credits: Auburn University, pp. 22, 25, 28; Bob Chwedyk, p. 42; John
Konstantaras, pp. 6, 9, 18, 31, 34, 38, 40, 47, 53, 57, 61, 65, 71, 76, 78, 80, 83, 90.

Cover Photo: AP/Wide World

Contents

Frank Thomas—the Big Hurt

Chapter 1

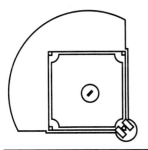

The Big Hurt

All eyes were on the batter's box when Frank Thomas stepped to the plate. The Chicago White Sox's first baseman stands six feet five and weighs 257 pounds. He draws a lot of attention before he even swings the bat, but taking his cuts at the plate is what he gets paid to do.

Thomas was expected to put on a good show at the home run hitting contest the day before the 1994 All-Star Game at Three Rivers Stadium in Pittsburgh. He had earned the nickname the Big Hurt for the power he showed at the plate, and Pittsburgh fans wanted to see for themselves what all the talk was about.

In a home run hitting contest he was sure to put his huge legs and muscular arms into every swing, so the real question was: Just how far can Thomas hit the ball?

Ken Griffey, Jr., of the Seattle Mariners and Barry Bonds of the San Francisco Giants were among major-league baseball's brightest stars gathered in Pittsburgh for the game. For those moments when Thomas stepped into the batter's box, though, they were just like the fans who had come to see their favorite players.

Standing up at the plate, Thomas could see from the numbers painted on the outfield wall that he would have to hit the ball 375 feet to left-center field in order to get a home run. It would take a drive of 400 feet to get the ball over the fence in center field. Thomas knew he wouldn't have any problem hitting the ball that far as long as he got his pitch.

He was right. Thomas blasted four balls over the wall, including two that absolutely amazed the sell-out crowd. One of the home runs traveled an incredible 512 feet, but Thomas was only warming up. He followed that home run with a blast that measured 519 feet. It was the longest home run ever hit at Three Rivers Stadium. Thomas showed that he was one of the strongest hitters in all of baseball.

When Thomas was finished hitting, the crowd gave him a standing ovation. They had come to be entertained, and Thomas put on a show they wouldn't soon forget.

In the 1994 All-Star Game, Thomas put on a good show for the fans in Pittsburgh. He hit a 519-foot homer in the pregame home run contest. It was the longest home run ever recorded in Three Rivers Stadium.

Everyone was expecting big things from Thomas at the All-Star Game. He finished the first half of the season with a great series against the Milwaukee Brewers to move his batting average up to .383. There was talk of a .400 season for Thomas.

No one had hit that high since Boston Red Sox great Ted Williams hit .406 in 1941. Thomas was one of the few current players who had a real chance to reach the .400 mark. Thomas hit a home run against the Tigers that almost hit the roof at Tiger Stadium. When Thomas took his place at first base in the bottom of the inning, Detroit first baseman Mickey Tettleton left him a note. Written in the dirt next to the first base bag was the word "Wow."[1] Said Detroit manager Sparky Anderson, "They ought to outlaw him from playing."[2]

Along with an impressive batting average, Thomas had 32 home runs and 78 runs batted in at the All-Star break. He had a chance to break a lot of records by the end of the season, but he didn't want to make any predictions. "The first half [of the season] is the first half," he said. "It's a long season. I'm just having fun hitting the ball the way I'm capable of hitting the ball."[3]

Thomas was picked by the fans as the American League's starting first baseman in the All-Star

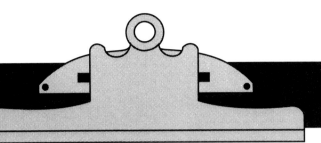

STATS

No major-league batter has had a .400 season since 1941. Following are the seven players who batted .403 or better since 1900. Three of these players had two .400 seasons.

Player	Team	Year	AB	H	Avg.
Ty Cobb	Detroit	1911	591	248	.420
Ty Cobb	Detroit	1912	533	227	.426
Harry Heilmann	Detroit	1923	524	211	.403
Rogers Hornsby	St. Louis	1924	536	227	.424
Rogers Hornsby	St. Louis	1925	504	203	.403
Joe Jackson	Cleveland	1911	571	233	.408
Nap Lajoie	Philadelphia	1901	543	229	.422
George Sisler	St. Louis	1920	631	257	.407
George Sisler	St. Louis	1922	586	246	.420
Ted Williams	Boston	1941	456	185	.406

Game for the first time in his young career. He did his part in an 8–7 loss to the National League.

Thomas drove in a run with a single to center field in the first inning. He drew a walk on four pitches in the fourth inning. In the sixth inning he singled to center field and later scored a run. He was replaced in the lineup by Texas's Will Clark at the end of the inning.

There would be much more to look forward to in Frank Thomas's young career. Not many players in the history of baseball had his combination of size and talent. Baseball was excited about Frank Thomas.

"I like this feeling," Thomas said. "And I don't feel I'm hitting over my head. I hit .400 in college. This was a level I needed to adjust to, but I think I've made that adjustment."[4]

Adjusting to Frank Thomas was going to be a big problem for American League pitchers for years to come.

Chapter 2

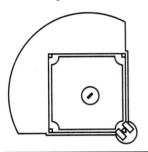

A Young Athlete

Frank Thomas was born May 27, 1968, in Columbus, Georgia. According to his grandmother, he was born to play ball.

Ida Bell Stroy loved to watch her young grandson run around in the yard. Although she didn't have much money, she spent what she could buying her grandson all the bats and balls that he needed. "This boy is going to be something someday," she said. "He loves to play ball."[1]

Columbus is a town of one hundred eighty thousand people. It's located on the Alabama-Georgia border, south of Atlanta. With its hot summers and mild winters, it was a great place for a kid who loves to be outside to grow up.

Thomas's mother, Charlie Mae, and his father, Frank Sr., worked hard to support their large family. Frank was the fifth child. Seven years later, his sister Pamela was born. Everyone was excited about the baby, including Frank. When he wasn't out playing ball, he liked to play with his baby sister. For so many years, Frank had been the baby in the family. Now Pamela was the one making everyone smile.

When she was two years old, Pamela became sick. When she didn't get better after a few days, her parents knew she needed to see a doctor. After tests were done, it was discovered that she had leukemia.

Pamela never got better. She died at the age of two and a half. Frank was nine when his sister died. He decided that the best way to honor his sister was to become "a great pro baseball player."[2]

So many young boys dream of being professional athletes. Frank promised to dedicate himself to making it. He worked out as hard as he could. He ate healthy food and cut back on sweets. He wasn't going to let anything stop him.

It was already clear by the time he was nine that Frank was a talented athlete. Not only was he bigger than other kids his age, but also he was as good as players that were two or three years older than he was. This was not just in his baseball game; Thomas was also an excellent basketball and football player. When Frank entered fifth grade he was given an athletic scholarship to attend Brookstone School, a private school in Columbus. He attended Brookstone for three years.[3]

Frank was beginning to see that being a good athlete could lead to some good opportunities for him. He knew he had a chance to make his dream of being a great baseball player come true. He believed in himself, and his family believed in him, too. His father once told him, "Don't let anybody ever tell you they're better than you. 'Cause they aren't."[4]

Frank Thomas couldn't wait to begin his high school career at Columbus High School, and Columbus High School baseball coach Bobby Howard couldn't wait to coach Thomas. He had seen him play baseball in the Babe Ruth League, and he knew Thomas was going to be a great addition to his team.

Frank elected not to try out for the baseball team his freshman year, but he was eager to make the team the next season. Because he was playing basketball, he wasn't able to join the rest of the team for practice in January.

Howard remembers the February afternoon Thomas showed up for his first practice. "He was wearing shorts and high-top tennis shoes,"

Howard said. "Our school sits about thirty feet beyond the outfield fence. Frank started hitting balls off the high school building. The coaches couldn't believe it. We said, 'Is this guy for real?' Frank really surprised me. I knew he was good, but I didn't know he was that good."

A couple of minor-league players from the Columbus area were working out with the high school team when Thomas came along. They couldn't believe how strong Thomas was. They were so impressed with his power they started calling him Boomer.

Howard became an important person in Thomas's life. Looking back, Thomas said Howard was the one who really pushed him to get in shape and to work hard in the weight room. Howard said he didn't push Thomas any harder than he did the rest of the kids. Thomas just had the desire and the skill to succeed.

"He just had a strong passion for the game of baseball," Howard said. "And that's a common passion between us. I think Frank would have taken batting practice all year round if the basketball and football coaches would have let him. That's something you just can't coach. Frank had that passion and drive."

Thomas hit .472 his first season, and Columbus

High School won the state championship. As he continued to work hard at the game, he continued to get better. When he was a junior in high school, the U.S. Pan-Am baseball team stopped in Columbus during the summer. Howard decided to get a team together to play a game. He found some college players home on vacation. The only high school player he asked to play was Frank Thomas. "We only had one hit when Frank came up late in the game," Howard said. "The pitcher decided to challenge Frank with a fastball, and Frank hit it about 450 feet for a home run. That was the only run we scored in the game. It meant something for Frank to play in that game, and I could tell that the home run did a lot for his confidence."

While baseball was clearly his favorite sport, Thomas continued to play basketball and football. He played well, and when he was a senior, he was picked to be a tight end for the all-state football team. Had he not injured his ankle during the basketball season, he might have been an all-state forward as well.

Thomas didn't disappoint anyone in his final baseball season. He hit .440 with 12 home runs and 52 runs batted in. Also among his 44 hits in 35 games were 10 doubles and 5 triples. The all-state tight end was also an all-state first baseman.

*Frank has played first base since high school. With the
White Sox, he has also been used as a designated hitter.*

Colleges all over the country were calling Thomas with scholarship offers. He decided to accept a football scholarship at Auburn University. Still, the major-league baseball draft would be held in June. Thomas had high hopes of being drafted. With the right offer, he would probably give up the football scholarship to play professional baseball.

Thomas waited next to the telephone the day of the draft, but the phone never rang. Hundreds of players were drafted, but he wasn't one of them. "I couldn't believe it when the phone never rang that day," he said. "I hit .400 in high school. I was already six foot four and 230 pounds by then. I couldn't believe no one would take a chance on me."[5]

One of the reasons Thomas wasn't drafted was that a lot of baseball scouts thought he was going to play football at Auburn. They didn't want to waste a pick on someone who wasn't going to play baseball. He said that all the scouts had to do was ask him. He would have told them how much he loved baseball.

Thomas was surprised and sad that June day. "I saw a lot of guys I played against get drafted," he said. "I knew they couldn't do what I could do."[6]

One month later, he packed his bags and headed for Auburn and the start of his first season of college football. He wasn't going to give up on baseball, though. The Auburn baseball coaches said he could try out for the team when football season ended.

Thomas couldn't wait. He was going to show what he could do on a baseball field.

Chapter 3

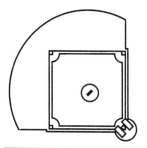

Auburn Star

When he packed his bags for Auburn University in the summer of 1986, Frank Thomas was joining a football program with a great history. The Tigers were often ranked among the top 20 teams in the country, and sent a number of players into the NFL. A year before Thomas enrolled in school, Auburn running back Bo Jackson won the Heisman Trophy, the award given to the best college football player in the country.

Thomas lined up at tight end for Auburn. At six feet four and 230 pounds, he had the size every team looks for at that position. By the end of summer practice, he had earned a spot as a backup. It is very difficult for a freshman to earn a starting position on a team as successful as Auburn, so Thomas's career was right on schedule.

Thomas appeared in three games his freshman

Auburn University offered Frank an athletic scholarship so that he could play on their football team.

season. He caught three passes for a total of 45 yards. The Tigers had another good year. They ended the season with a win over the University of Southern California in the Citrus Bowl. The win gave Auburn a record of 10–2. The Tigers finished the year rated as the sixth-best team in college football.

As expected, Thomas began working out with the Auburn baseball team after the football season ended. The Tigers were coming off a season in which they won 31 games and lost 24, and Coach Hal Baird was looking forward to getting a look at the big freshman from Columbus, Georgia.

Baird stood behind the batting cage as Thomas stepped up to the plate for batting practice. Thomas swung at the first pitch and hit a sharp line drive toward shortstop. Baird turned to one of his assistant coaches and said, "There's our No. 4 hitter for the next three years."[1]

As Thomas continued to swing the bat, Baird saw a hitter who obviously knew what he was doing. His timing was not where it would be if he had been practicing with everyone else, but Thomas was making good contact on almost every pitch. "The rest of our kids had been practicing all fall while Frank was playing football," Baird said. "But in two days Frank was further

FACT

Auburn University, founded in 1856, is located in Auburn, Alabama. It has produced a number of superb athletes including Bo Jackson, Frank Thomas, and Charles Barkley.

along than most of them. His transition from football to baseball was amazing."[2]

Thomas made the team as the starting first baseman and cleanup hitter, and he didn't let his team down. Thomas set an Auburn record with 21 home runs, including 2 grand slams. In a season that included sixty games, Thomas collected 68 RBIs and scored 56 runs. He was selected to the Southeastern Conference All-Star team.

Thomas's success made him a well-known student on the Auburn campus. One of the people he got to know was Bo Jackson, who often returned to the campus to work out after leaving to play football in the National Football League.

While Jackson had many great days on the football field ahead of him, Thomas's football career had come to an end. Baseball was his game, and he decided to devote all of his time to working toward a major-league career.

According to Baird, both Jackson and Thomas made the right decision. "Bo was a football player playing baseball," he said. "Frank was a baseball player. Frank studied baseball. He remembered how guys pitched him."

"Playing football for Auburn was a whole new world for me," Thomas said. "I had always thought I had worked hard. But while I was there

Thomas was chosen to play on the U.S. Baseball Team in the Pan American Games of 1988.

I learned what hard work means. Just to be competitive, I had to really throw the weights around. And when I showed up for baseball practice that spring I could tell my power had doubled."[3]

Auburn football coach Pat Dye hated to see Thomas go, but he kept him on football scholarship, although he only played baseball. Dye said a number of times that Thomas had the talent to play tight end in the National Football League if he had stayed with football.

Part of Thomas's decision had to do with the number of injuries football players suffer. He didn't want to risk doing anything that would cost him a shot at becoming a professional baseball player. He also knew that it was unusual for a big athlete to choose baseball over football. "A lot of big guys lean toward football because the season's shorter," Thomas said. "Sixteen weeks, that's it. Baseball lingers on for six, seven months, and it's every day. Some big guys don't think they can handle it."[4]

Thomas couldn't get enough baseball. He came back as a sophomore with another outstanding season for Auburn. His .385 batting average led the Southeastern Conference as he was again named to the conference All-Star team.

Recognized as one of the best college baseball

players in the country, Thomas was selected to play on the U.S. Pan-Am team in the summer of 1988. He responded by hitting .339 with 2 home runs and 15 runs batted in.

Looking ahead to his junior year at Auburn, Thomas made up his mind to make it his best season yet. He would once again be eligible for the major-league draft, and he was going to make the scouts notice him this time.

The 1989 season proved to be a great one for Auburn and its star first baseman. The Tigers won the Southeastern Conference for the first time since 1978 and advanced to the NCAA Atlantic Regional.

Thomas led the conference with a .403 batting average. His 83 runs batted in also led the conference, and he was second with 19 home runs. Opposing pitchers were finding out that it wasn't much fun to pitch to him. He was hit 10 times by pitches and was walked 73 times, an Auburn record.

Thomas was named the Southeastern Conference Most Valuable Player. The *Sporting News* put him on its All-America team. There was no doubt that Thomas would be a top draft choice in the upcoming draft.

Thomas set eight school records at Auburn,

FACT

The Pan American Sports Games, better known as the Pan Am Games, were first held in 1951. Modeled after the Olympics, participants are limited to the countries of the Western Hemisphere.

Thomas knew his junior year would be his last at Auburn. He led the conference with a .403 batting average and 83 RBIs.

including home runs in a career (49) and RBIs in a career (205). Along with being the school's best power hitter, he had a career batting average of .382.

"From the first couple of days I saw him I thought he was the best I had ever seen," Baird said. "His eye [for hitting], his knowledge of the strike zone, his ability to hit the ball the other way. He had those things the day he got to Auburn."[5]

Added Baird, "We went through a period in the Southeastern Conference where we had some terrific players. Will Clark [of Mississippi State and the Texas Rangers], Rafael Palmeiro [of Mississippi State and the Baltimore Orioles], Ben McDonald [of Louisiana State and the Orioles] and you can go on and on. And none compared to Frank."[6]

Chapter 4

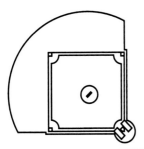

Rookie

There was one thing sure to happen in the 1989 baseball draft: Ben McDonald was going to be the top pick. Everyone agreed that the six-foot-seven pitcher from Louisiana State University was ready to pitch in the majors. The Baltimore Orioles owned the first pick, and they weren't going to let McDonald get away.

Once again, Frank Thomas found himself waiting for the telephone to ring on the day of the draft, but this time he knew he wouldn't have to wait long. The Chicago White Sox, picking seventh, were disappointed when the Philadelphia Phillies selected outfielder Jeff Jackson with the fourth pick.

Jackson was a high school star from Chicago, and the White Sox were hoping he would one day play professional baseball in front of his hometown

The Chicago White Sox were looking for strong hitters in the 1989 baseball draft. With the seventh pick in the first round, they drafted Frank.

fans. Some of the disappointment was taken away when the White Sox were able to select Thomas.

The White Sox, a team known for developing good young pitchers, were looking to add some power to their lineup. Thomas showed at Auburn that he had as much power as anyone already playing in the major leagues. If he continued to develop, he had a chance to be exactly what the White Sox were looking for.

Al Goldis, the White Sox's director of scouting, pointed out that Thomas had hit some 500-foot home runs off Ben McDonald in college. McDonald's fastball had been clocked at ninety-five miles per hour, which is well above the average in the major leagues.

Still, the Sox knew that there was a big difference between hitting for power in college and doing it against major-league pitching. College hitters also had to adjust to using wooden bats in professional baseball after using aluminum bats in college. The ball goes farther and comes off the bat faster with an aluminum bat. Thomas was more than just a power hitter. He had good skills as a hitter, too.

After signing his first professional contract, Thomas was sent to Florida to play for the White Sox's rookie team in Sarasota. He appeared in only seventeen games, but he showed he was ready for minor-league pitching. He batted .365 and was moved up to the White Sox's Class A farm team in Sarasota.

Thomas's batting averaged dipped to .277 at the Class A level, but he connected for 4 home runs and drove in 30 runs in 55 games. The White Sox were excited about their new hitting prospect. Thomas was ready for every challenge that came his way.

With his first season of professional baseball behind him, Thomas looked forward to the 1990 season. He would be playing for the White Sox's Class AA team in Birmingham, Alabama. He would be playing close to home, and he also knew he was moving closer to playing in the major leagues.

Thomas knew that baseball had changed in recent years. Young players used to have to move all the way up to Class AAA ball before getting called up to the majors, but now, the best prospects usually got called up after playing one season of Class AA ball.

There are a number of reasons for the change. One of the main reasons is that teams are drafting more players out of college than they used to. A high school player usually needs more time in the minor leagues, but some college stars move from college baseball right into the major leagues.

Thomas practices jumping. Being able to reach up and catch a high line drive could save a game.

When Thomas reported to spring training, he knew he could be less than a year away from joining the White Sox. The minor-leaguers work out with the major-leaguers early in spring training, and Thomas was too big and too talented to go unnoticed.

Once the spring training games began, Thomas's name was coming up a lot during conversations in the dugout and in the stands. As a first-round draft pick, he had a lot to live up to, and he was doing it. In seven spring training games, he batted .529 with 2 home runs and 7 RBIs. Those who watched him swing the bat were wondering if he was ready to open the season as the White Sox's starting first baseman.

Hitting was only half of Thomas's responsibilities. The White Sox coaches were all in agreement that he needed to improve his defense at first base before he would be ready to play in the major leagues, so it came as no real surprise when he was sent to Birmingham.

"Frank is going to have to keep working on his defense," said Birmingham manager Ken Berry. "I don't think he received a lot of knowledge of fielding in college. There it was, 'Take the bat and hit the ball.' So it may take a while."[1]

Thomas adjusted to AA pitching with little

trouble. By the beginning of summer he was considered by many to be the best hitter in all of minor-league baseball. The only real question was how long he would be in the minor leagues.

The White Sox had plenty of first basemen on their roster, but none of them were hitting very well. Ron Kittle and Greg Walker were two veterans who had been stars in the past, but both appeared to be nearing the end of their careers. Carlos Martinez was a promising young hitter, but he wasn't consistent enough to be considered an everyday player. White Sox manager Jeff Torborg gave them all an opportunity to play, but no one showed enough to earn the job.

Meanwhile, Thomas was hitting .323 with 18 home runs and 71 RBIs through 109 games at Birmingham. Pitchers were finding out that it was safer to walk him when he came up with runners on base than to give him a chance to swing the bat.

Thomas had already drawn over 100 walks and was on his way to breaking the league record for walks in a season. Although he wanted to get his swings, he wasn't about to give in to the pitchers and swing at bad pitches. "It's nothing that can be taught," said Thomas of his patience at the plate. "It's natural instinct—just being picky, having your own hitting zone. If it's not there, if it's not what I want, I just won't swing at it."[2]

"A power hitter with a good eye like that is hard to find," said White Sox scout Larry Monroe. "I'm sure a lot of the pitchers down there are afraid of him."[3]

On August 2, 1990, those same pitchers waved good-bye to Thomas with smiles on their faces. He received a call from the White Sox to join them for a weekend series in Milwaukee with the Brewers. "I was shocked," Thomas said. "They said, 'Clean out your locker, you're going to Milwaukee.'"[4] The White Sox couldn't wait any longer for someone to earn the first base job. Walker was released from the team. Kittle had already been traded to Baltimore for outfielder Phil Bradley.

"It's my time, I guess," Thomas said. "If I didn't think I was ready, I don't belong in baseball. I knew it was just a matter of time. So I didn't feel nervous when I got the news . . ."[5]

The White Sox obviously felt Thomas was ready. Said general manager Larry Himes, "He'll be a power source for the White Sox."[6]

Thomas wasn't going to worry about hitting home runs, however. His goal was to be a .300 hitter. With his size and strength, he knew the home runs would come if he hit the ball solidly.

FACT

The Chicago White Sox played their first season in 1901. They have appeared in four World Series—1906, 1917, 1919, and 1959. Their last win was in 1917.

In 1990, the White Sox called Frank Thomas up to the major leagues.

The White Sox didn't waste any time putting Thomas into the lineup. He played first base in the first game of a doubleheader against Milwaukee the day he joined the team. While he didn't get a hit in four at-bats, Thomas's groundout in the ninth inning scored the winning run from third base.

The White Sox won Game 2 of the doubleheader with Thomas watching from the bench, but he was back in the lineup the next day. Once again he helped lead the White Sox to a victory.

Thomas came to the plate in the seventh inning with the Sox trailing the Brewers, 2–1. There were two runners on base, so he knew Milwaukee pitcher Mark Knudson would be trying to throw strikes.

Thomas made good contact, sending a drive to right field. The ball bounced off the top of the wall as two runs scored. Thomas pulled up with his first major-league triple.

"If the wind hadn't been blowing in it would have been gone," said White Sox manager Jeff Torborg. "The guys who saw him hit the ball over the scoreboard in Birmingham know he's got power."[7]

Thomas said that when he stepped up to the plate, he pretended he was in Birmingham. "I

Frank Thomas smiles in practice. White Sox fans were giving credit to the young first baseman for adding spark to the team.

know it's a different situation," he said, "but I was a little nervous."[8]

The White Sox went on to win the game 6–2 for their third straight win since Thomas was called up from the minors. The big first baseman was getting credit for adding a spark to the team.

After going hitless in his first game, Thomas put together a seven-game hitting streak, and the White Sox kept winning as they moved back into the race for first place in the American League West.

As things turned out, the White Sox didn't win their division, finishing third. They did win 95 games, a great season for a young team, and Thomas had a great season for a young player.

While the White Sox were saying hello to their new star, they were saying good-bye to their old ballpark. Comiskey Park had been the White Sox's home for over eighty years. With a new ballpark being built across the street, 1990 would be the last season in baseball's oldest ballpark.

The Seattle Mariners met the White Sox on September 30, in the last game at the old Comiskey Park. A crowd of 42,849 turned out for the historic event. The White Sox closed the doors with a 2–1 win over the Mariners. Thomas played a part by scoring the last run ever at the old Comiskey. He came across on a triple by Dan Pasqua.

FACT

The old Comiskey Park had been the home of the Chicago White Sox since 1910. Before it was demolished in 1990, it was the oldest stadium still in use in the major leagues.

It didn't take long for Thomas to put his name down in the White Sox history books. He scored the last run ever at the old Comiskey Park, and finished the season with the best batting average of any White Sox player in forty-eight years.

The White Sox ended their season with high hopes for 1991, and Thomas was a big reason why. He played in 60 games, batting .330 with 7 home runs and 31 RBIs. His batting average was the highest by a White Sox player in forty-eight years.

While he didn't play in enough games to get into the race for Rookie of the Year, Thomas did enough to make everyone in baseball see him as a superstar ready to break loose.

Chapter 5

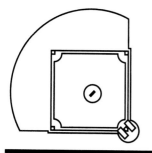

A New Era?

White Sox officials had pointed toward the 1991 season for a long time. A fun year was expected because of the opening of the new ballpark. But what could be better than to be in a pennant race as well?

With that in mind, they tried to make sure that White Sox fans had an exciting ballclub to come out to watch. Frank Thomas was a big part of that, but the White Sox were putting together a solid ballclub in all areas. Robin Ventura was one of the best young third basemen in all of baseball, and a pitching staff that included Jack McDowell and young Alex Fernandez figured to keep the White Sox in a lot of ballgames.

The White Sox made a major trade in the off-season, too, trading left fielder Ivan Calderon to the Montreal Expos for left fielder Tim Raines.

Calderon had been one of the best power hitters on the team, but with the addition of Thomas, the Sox could afford to give up Calderon's power.

Raines gave the White Sox a leadoff hitter and someone who could steal bases. In his ten seasons with Montreal, Raines batted .300 or better five times, and averaged 62 stolen bases a season. He led the National League in stolen bases four times, including in 1983, when he stole 90 bases.

For added excitement, the White Sox signed a new designated hitter. Thomas was going to be joined in the batting order by another former Auburn Tiger, Bo Jackson.

Jackson was still recovering from a serious hip injury he suffered while playing football, but the White Sox were willing to wait until he was ready to play baseball again. Playing for the Los Angeles Raiders, Jackson was injured during a playoff game against the Cincinnati Bengals. He was carrying the football on a long run down the sideline when he was tackled from behind. He fell backward, and the muscle was pulled away from the hip.

Jackson soon found out that his football career was over. As for baseball, he was determined to make a comeback. It would take a lot of sweat and a lot of pain, but Jackson was willing to put in the time. He knew he would miss most of the season, but he promised to be back to help the Sox win baseball games.

The White Sox opened their new ballpark on April 18 with an afternoon game against the Detroit Tigers. A sellout crowd of forty-two thousand was guaranteed. The White Sox had opened the season on the road and won five of their first six games. Star pitcher Jack McDowell was set to face the Tigers after winning his first two starts of the season.

It didn't turn out to be much of a game, at least for the home team. The Tigers bombed the White Sox 16–0. It was the worst home opener in the history of the White Sox.

McDowell didn't make it through the third inning. The Tigers hit him for 6 runs in the third, including a three-run home run by big Cecil Fielder. McDowell's replacements didn't do much better. Detroit scored 10 runs in the fourth inning to put the game away. Sox fans were left to wander around the new ballpark, and to look across the street where the old Comiskey Park was being torn down.

It took a while for the Sox to get used to their new home. A total of six home runs were hit by opposing teams at the new Comiskey before the

Thomas continued to write history with the White Sox when he became the first on his team to hit a home run at the new Comiskey Park.

White Sox got their first one. Frank Thomas put his name in the history books when he hit it in the first night game at new Comiskey.

Thomas's two-run home run, his first of the season, gave the White Sox an 8–7 win over Baltimore. "I was just happy to get it out of the way," he said.[1]

Thomas didn't stop there. He developed into the power hitter everyone knew he could be. On

FACT

Chicago, the home of two major-league baseball teams, has a long baseball tradition. For three consecutive years (1906–1908) Chicago was home to a World Series Champion. In 1906, the Cubs and the White Sox met in an all-Chicago World Series.

Team	Chicago Cubs	Chicago White Sox
League	National League	American League
Ballpark	Wrigley Field	Comiskey Park
Founded	1876	1901
World Series Appearances	10 (1906–8, 1910, 1918, 1929, 1932, 1935, 1938, 1945)	4 (1906, 1917, 1919, 1959)
World Series Wins	2 (1907, 1908)	2 (1906, 1917)

May 24 he set a career high with 5 RBIs in an 11–1 win over Oakland. Despite playing with a sore shoulder, Thomas was leading the White Sox in home runs and RBIs.

"You have people say to you in the minors, 'Nobody plays like that in the major leagues, the pitching is too good,'" Thomas said. "I told people, 'I believe I can.' A lot of guys, when they get up here, are overwhelmed by the big crowds, the TV, the media everywhere. It didn't bother me. I'd been around it at Auburn. Playing football in front of 80,000 people really helped."[2]

Thanks to Thomas's hot bat, the White Sox stayed in the race for first place in the American League West as the month of August approached. Thomas hit homers in back-to-back games in Toronto to help the Sox's winning streak reach six games.

Thomas continued to be a red-hot hitter for the month of August. He batted .373 with 8 home runs and 27 runs batted in. He was selected the American League Player of the Month.

It wasn't enough to keep the White Sox in a pennant race. They won only 12 games in August, losing 18, and fell eight and a half games behind the first-place Minnesota Twins.

Bo Jackson made his White Sox debut on

September 1, and he shared the headlines with Thomas. "I'm excited to be back," Jackson said. "Most people thought I'd never play baseball again, and here I'm back in eight months. I'm just going to go out and have fun."[3]

Thomas, who was both happy for Jackson and thrilled to have him in the lineup, celebrated with his 100th RBI of the season. Thomas reached the magic number by hitting a three-run home run in a 6–1 win over the Cleveland Indians. "All I'm trying to do is stay consistent," Thomas said. "I did the same thing [drive in 100 runs] at the minor-league level. This is just another level. I'm hitting a few more home runs, but basically I'm the same Frank."[4]

The White Sox set a new team attendance record when 2,934,154 fans turned out at new Comiskey Park. The season was considered a disappointment, however, when the White Sox finished eight games out of first place with an 87–75 record.

More changes were coming: Manager Jeff Torborg decided to leave after the season to manage the New York Mets. Gene Lamont, a coach with the Pittsburgh Pirates, was hired to take his place. Lamont knew he was joining a team that had a good chance to make it to the playoffs in 1992.

Thomas finished the season with a .318 batting average. He was fifth in the American League with 32 home runs and fifth in the league with 109 runs batted in. He joined former first baseman Dick Allen as the only White Sox to hit over .300, hit 30 or more home runs, and drive in over 100 runs in a season. He also set a White Sox record with 138 walks for the season.

Thomas finished third in voting for American League Most Valuable Player behind the winner, Baltimore's Cal Ripken, Jr., and Cecil Fielder of the Detroit Tigers. It was a terrific year for a player who was playing his first full season in the major leagues.

Thomas was forced to play one hundred and one games as designated hitter because of the shoulder injury that bothered him from early in the season. The injury didn't allow him to throw the ball well enough to play first base, but doctors told him that rest would leave the shoulder completely healthy for the 1992 season.

The White Sox knew they had to get better. With that in mind, general manager Ron Schueler spent a lot of time during the winter trying to make a trade. The White Sox were interested in trading for Pittsburgh superstar Barry Bonds. A player of Bonds's ability is not often available in a trade, but the Pirates weren't able to afford his salary. The Pirates were looking for young talent in return, and wanted Thomas as part of any trade with the White Sox. No deal: Thomas wasn't going anywhere.

Spring training of 1992 brought one of the trades Schueler hoped to make. The White Sox sent promising outfielder Sammy Sosa to the Chicago Cubs for outfielder/designated hitter George Bell. Bell, a proven hitter, was added to give the Sox someone to bat after Thomas. The feeling was that if teams were going to continue to walk Thomas, the Sox would have Bell there to make them pay.

The White Sox started the season with eight wins in their first twelve games. They reached mid-May as a first-place team, and Thomas and Bell were a big part of their success. Thomas put together a nine-game hitting streak and, after hitting .435 with 3 home runs and 9 runs batted in, he was named American League Player of the Week.

Teammate Robin Ventura was certainly impressed with what he saw of Thomas. He said Thomas had a chance to be the best player in the history of the game.

Bell, meanwhile, led the White Sox with 5 home runs, 25 RBIs, and a .324 batting average.

The White Sox struggled to a third place finish in 1992, but Frank Thomas kept on hitting.

As had been hoped, Thomas and Bell were as tough a one-two punch as there was in baseball.

The good times didn't last for the White Sox. They ended May with six straight losses to fall into fourth place in the division. By the end of June, they were seven games back. It was clear to everyone that the Sox were not going to be a playoff team.

When Thomas earned Player of the Week honors again at the end of July, he was the only member of the starting lineup hitting over .300. The Sox had fallen to 47–50, twelve and a half games behind the Minnesota Twins.

While he was disappointed in the team's performance, Thomas kept on hitting. He had one of the biggest days of his young career on September 16. He knocked out 5 hits in 5 at-bats in a 9–6 win over the New York Yankees. Thomas and Bell both reached the 100 RBI mark that week, but the Sox weren't good enough to challenge for a pennant. They played much better late in the season and finished with an 86–76 record—but it was only good enough for third place.

Thomas hit .323 for the season to finish third in the American League batting race. His 115 RBIs also were third best in the league. While his home run total dipped to 24, he tied for the league lead in doubles with 46. Thomas became only the second White Sox player to hit 20 or more home runs and drive in 100 or more runs in two straight seasons. Eddie Robinson had done it in 1951–1952.

Although the White Sox had another disappointing season, Thomas continued to work to grow as a hitter. Although he was only twenty-four years old, the White Sox knew they had a player to build a championship team around.

Chapter 6

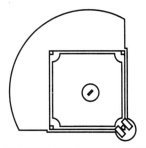

The White Sox were eager to put the disappointment of the 1992 season behind them when they went to spring training in February 1993. They liked their team, which included a key free-agent addition. Veteran outfielder Ellis Burks gave them another good hitter in the middle of their lineup.

Burks had established himself as a solid center fielder in six seasons with the Boston Red Sox. He had a disappointing season in 1992, however. A back injury allowed him to play in only sixty-six games. The Red Sox decided not to offer him a new contract. The White Sox were happy to add him to their lineup, but they knew they were taking a gamble. There still were questions about Burks's back.

A young pitching staff had gained another

Thomas looked forward to the 1993 season determined to help his team earn a spot in the pennant race.

year of valuable experience and was sure to make an impact as the White Sox set out to win their first division title in ten years. The same, of course, was being said of Frank Thomas.

Thomas agreed to a new contract early in the season. The deal was worth $29 million over four years. It made him one of the highest-paid players in baseball. "Money never motivated me before, and it won't," he said. "I play this game to have fun and be a good ballplayer."[1]

The White Sox did not begin the season like a team considered good enough to win a championship. A 1–0 loss to Toronto on April 25 left them with an 8–9 record. They were tied for third place, four and a half games out of first.

They followed that with a six-game winning streak, however, and after losing two games, the White Sox put together another six-game winning streak. By the first week of May, they were in first place. Thomas did his part, collecting 21 RBIs in April, the most by a White Sox in nearly twenty years.

The White Sox hit a bad period at the end of May. They lost six games in a row, and from that point until the end of June they were unable to play as well as they knew they could play.

July turned out to be a different story all

FACT

The first All-Star Game was played in Comiskey Park in 1933. Frank Thomas is now bringing back some glory to the White Sox. He was selected to the American League team each year from 1993 to 1997. Following is the run down on the All-Star Games since 1986.

Year	Winner	Location
1986	American (3-2)	Houston, Tex.
1987	National (2-0)	Oakland, Calif.
1988	American (2-1)	Cincinnati, Ohio
1989	American (5-3)	Anaheim, Calif.
1990	American (2-0)	Chicago, Ill.
1991	American (4-2)	Toronto, Ontario
1992	American (13-6)	San Diego, Calif.
1993	American (9-3)	Baltimore, Md.
1994	National (8-7)	Pittsburgh, Pa.
1995	National (3-2)	Arlington, Tex.
1996	National (6-0)	Philadelphia, Pa.
1997	American (3-1)	Cleveland, Ohio
1998	American (13-8)	Denver, Colo.

Though the American League has the most All-Star Game wins since 1986, the National League is leading the all-time race with 40 wins.

together, and Thomas was a big reason why. On July 11, he hit 2 home runs and drove in 5 runs as the White Sox beat Baltimore 11–5. The win gave the White Sox a one-game lead in the division at the All-Star break over the Texas Rangers and Kansas City Royals.

Thomas certainly earned his spot on the American League All-Star team for the game in Baltimore. He did not start in the game but came through with a pinch-hit single in his only at-bat. Thomas and the White Sox were the subjects of a lot of talk at the All-Star game. The Sox had the lead in the American League West Division, and a lot of people believed they could hold on to it.

When the second half of the season began, the White Sox picked up right where they left off. They won five games in a row to open up a three-game lead in the division. White Sox players found themselves in the position they always had wanted to be in. Coming to the ballpark was fun, and they couldn't wait to get there. They were having fun on the field and off it.

The players added a Ping-Pong table to the middle of the clubhouse, and just about everyone enjoyed playing. Thomas, Bo Jackson, shortstop Ozzie Guillen, catcher Ron Karkovice, and pitcher Kirk McCaskill were among those players

The White Sox worked hard in 1993 to become one of the best teams in baseball. As the end of the season neared, it looked like their hard work might pay off.

who made Ping-Pong a part of their everyday routine. There were winners and losers in Ping-Pong, but the White Sox didn't do much losing on the field. They ended the month of July with another five-game winning streak to push their lead in the division to four games.

Thomas hit a two-run homer on July 31 as the White Sox beat Seattle, 13–10. He hit .345 for the month of July with 25 RBIs in twenty-six games.

By the end of August, the White Sox were one of the best teams in baseball, and Thomas was almost everyone's choice as the most dangerous hitter in baseball. He earned his third Player of the Month award by hitting .333 with 10 home runs and 26 runs batted in. "I've had a great year," he said. "My stats are there. But we're playing as a team. We're out to win it together."[2]

The White Sox led the American League West by five and a half games. The Sox and their fans were preparing for a celebration on the South Side of Chicago. When the Sox split a doubleheader with the Texas Rangers at Comiskey Park on September 26, they clinched at least a tie for the American League West Division.

The Seattle Mariners came to Chicago for a game the next night. The White Sox had a chance to win the division in front of their own fans. They sent left-hander Wilson Alvarez to the mound in search of his seventh straight win. Alvarez pitched well, but the White Sox fell behind, 2–1, after five innings. In the bottom of the sixth, Bo Jackson came to the plate with two outs and two runners on base. After working the count to 3–0 against Seattle's Dave Fleming, Jackson hit a high fly ball to left field. To Jackson's surprise, the ball kept carrying. When the ball cleared the wall for a three-run home run, Comiskey Park exploded.

The White Sox now needed only six more outs to clinch the division title. Alvarez gave way to relief pitcher Kirk McCaskill, and McCaskill did his job. When Seattle's Dave Valle flew out to Ellis Burks in right field, the celebration began.

Fireworks exploded over the center field scoreboard. After saluting the crowd on the field, the players headed for the clubhouse, where they hugged and screamed and sprayed champagne all over each other.

Thomas was thrilled to have clinched the division for more than the obvious reasons. He had hurt his elbow a week earlier, and he was still in a lot of pain. He would now be able to rest the final week of the season. His next big game would be the start of the American League playoffs against the Toronto Blue Jays.

The Blue Jays were a very good team. Like the White Sox, they had good pitching and a superstar hitter. Right fielder Joe Carter was Toronto's answer to Frank Thomas.

The series opened at Comiskey Park, but Toronto felt right at home. The Blue Jays beat the White Sox, 7–3. Blue Jays pitcher Juan Guzman limited the Sox to six hits. Toronto hitters exploded for seventeen hits and knocked White Sox starter Jack McDowell around. It was not the kind of night the record crowd of 46,246 was expecting.

Game 2 was more of the same for the White Sox. Toronto pitcher Dave Stewart kept the Sox's bats from doing any damage, and the Blue Jays won, 3–1. Chicago sports fans weren't happy with the outcome of the game, but it was not the worst news they got that day. Michael Jordan had held a press conference earlier in the day to announce that he was leaving the Bulls and retiring from professional basketball. Jordan was watching Game 1 from a private box at Comiskey Park when word got out about his retirement.

With the win in Game 2, Toronto now needed only two more wins to earn a trip to the World Series. Thomas knew it was time he started hitting.

The series moved to the SkyDome in Toronto,

Looking back on the 1993 season, Thomas called it "a learning experience." But it was much more than that for Thomas—he won his first MVP award.

and the White Sox got their offense going. They scored 5 runs in the third inning and went on to win, 6–1. It was Thomas who gave the White Sox the lead they never lost, he drove in a run with a single and later scored a run himself.

Thomas was walked intentionally in the fourth inning to load the bases. White Sox third baseman Robin Ventura came through with a sacrifice fly to score the White Sox's sixth run. That was more than enough for White Sox pitcher Wilson Alvarez.

The White Sox weren't satisfied with just winning one game, and they proved it in Game 4. They beat the Blue Jays, 7–4, to tie the best-of-seven series at two apiece. Thomas tied the game with a home run in the sixth inning. The blast was measured at 433 feet. The Sox went on to score two more runs in the inning to take control of the game.

Thomas was walked intentionally in the first inning. It was the eighth time he had walked in the series, setting a new American League record for the playoffs. The Blue Jays felt that in many situations, walking Thomas was safer than letting him hit.

They didn't have much to worry about in Game 5, though. Thomas didn't get a hit in three at-bats, as the White Sox lost, 5–3. The White Sox were going home to Comiskey Park knowing they needed to win or their season was over.

The Blue Jays opened up an early 2–0 lead in Game 6. The White Sox answered with a pair of runs of their own, with Thomas collecting one of the RBIs. Toronto scored a run in the fourth inning, and it stayed a 3–2 game until the ninth. Toronto scored three times to take a 6–2 lead.

The White Sox came up with one run in the ninth inning but had to settle for second best in the American League in 1993. The White Sox's dream of going to the World Series for the first time since 1959 was over.

"It was a learning experience for us," Thomas said of the long season. "We'll be back next season and we'll be ready to take the next step up. We'll just have to shake it off right now and come back next year with a positive attitude in spring training. We got a taste of it this year, and we know how sweet it is."[3]

Thomas didn't let himself down in his first chance to play in the playoffs. He hit .353 to go along with 10 walks. As expected, he won the Most Valuable Player Award in the American League. He received all twenty-eight first-place votes, making him the tenth player in history to

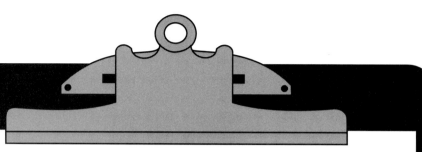

STATS

Frank Thomas won the American League MVP award two years in a row. Following is a list of the MVPs in both leagues since 1986:

	American League		National League
1986	Roger Clemens, Boston	1986	Mike Schmidt, Philadelphia
1987	George Bell, Toronto	1987	Andre Dawson, Chicago
1988	Jose Canseco, Oakland	1988	Kirk Gibson, Los Angeles
1989	Robin Yount, Milwaukee	1989	Kevin Mitchell, San Francisco
1990	Rickey Henderson, Oakland	1990	Barry Bonds, Pittsburgh
1991	Cal Ripken, Jr., Baltimore	1991	Terry Pendleton, Atlanta
1992	Dennis Eckersley, Oakland	1992	Barry Bonds, Pittsburgh
1993	Frank Thomas, Chicago	1993	Barry Bonds, San Francisco
1994	Frank Thomas, Chicago	1994	Jeff Bagwell, Houston
1995	Mo Vaughn, Boston	1995	Barry Larkin, Cincinnati
1996	Juan Gonzalez, Texas	1996	Ken Caminiti, San Diego
1997	Ken Griffey, Jr., Seattle	1997	Larry Walker, Colorado

be a unanimous winner. Thomas became the first White Sox to win the MVP Award since Dick Allen won it in 1972. "I'm very happy right now," he said on the day the award was announced. "This is the biggest day of my career."[4]

Thomas hit 41 home runs for the 1993 season, breaking the team record of 37 set by Dick Allen. His 128 runs batted in were only ten short of the team record set in 1936. It was the kind of season the White Sox were hoping to get from Thomas and the kind of season a lot of people were expecting.

"He drove in so many big runs for us," said White Sox manager Gene Lamont. "I'd hate to think what it would have been like without him."[5]

With the new contract Thomas signed, the White Sox weren't going to have to worry about playing without him for years to come. They were thinking instead about winning a World Series with Thomas, and they felt they had a great chance to do it in 1994.

Chapter 7

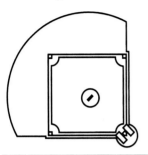

Superstar

When spring training began in February 1994 Frank Thomas was one of the biggest stories in all of baseball, but the White Sox had a bigger one in their own training camp: Michael Jordan.

Having retired from professional basketball the year before, Jordan announced that his new goal was to make it as a major-league baseball player. Since Jerry Reinsdorf owned both the Chicago Bulls and the White Sox, Jordan was able to work out a deal to join the White Sox farm system.

Jordan clearly had a lot of work ahead of him if he was ever going to make it to the major leagues, but just being in uniform was enough to make him a major story.

Some people wondered if Jordan's presence would be a distraction to the other players. After all, the White Sox had a team that looked like it

After his retirement from the NBA in 1993, basketball superstar Michael Jordan was signed by the White Sox. He joined Frank Thomas in batting practice at the 1994 spring training camp. The White Sox later assigned him to their farm team in Birmingham, Alabama.

had a chance to win it all. Things eventually settled down, though, when Jordan was assigned to Class AA Birmingham. The White Sox were looking forward to what promised to be a great season.

Thomas received a lot of attention due to his season in 1993, but he preferred to think about bigger and better things. "I never look back," he said. "I'm playing this game because I love it. I'm like a kid. Last year was my piece of history and no one can ever take that away from me."[1]

Thomas was excited about two free-agent additions to the White Sox' lineup, designated hitter Julio Franco and right fielder Darrin Jackson. Franco, a career .300 hitter, gave the White Sox a proven hitter to bat behind Thomas. Jackson came in to replace Ellis Burks, who had signed with the Colorado Rockies.

With baseball changing to three divisions in each league, the White Sox and Cleveland Indians were picked to fight for the crown in the American League Central. There was one thing, however, that could keep the 1994 season from being a great one. The season began with the threat of a strike by the players if they couldn't agree to a new union contract with the owners.

After playing good but not great baseball the

first two months of the season, the White Sox had the lead in the Central Division by two and a half games. The month of June brought some long days, though. After losing four straight games to Minnesota, the Sox dropped into a tie for first place.

They came home for ten games, and after beating Oakland, they lost the next two games to fall into third place. On June 16 it was clear that the Sox were not a happy bunch of players. After the Sox lost to California, one of the players went back to the clubhouse and expressed his anger. He picked up a bat and smashed the Ping-Pong table into pieces. No one ever said who did it, but the move seemed to wake the team up.

The White Sox made their move in July. They won nineteen games during the month. They lost only ten and moved to the top of the Central division. A number of players were playing well for the White Sox, but none better than Thomas.

"It seems like we talk about Frank every night," said White Sox manager Gene Lamont.[2] On July 9, Thomas led the White Sox past Milwaukee for their fifth straight win. Thomas had 3 hits, including a home run, and drove in 5 runs as the Sox won, 11–7. He took over the lead among American League hitters as his average rose to .384. He also was second in home runs with 32 and second in RBIs with 78 as the All-Star break approached.

"The first half is the first half," Thomas said. "It's a long season and I have to keep doing what I'm doing."[3]

The White Sox held on to first place as the day the players picked to go on strike drew near. On August 10, the Sox beat Oakland, 2–1, and the strike began. "It doesn't feel like the end," Thomas said. "You never know what's going to happen."[4]

While there was hope for a while that the strike would end in time for the season to resume, it didn't happen. The White Sox ended the season one game ahead of Cleveland in the American League Central, but there would be no playoffs, and for the first time since 1904, no World Series.

As expected, Thomas won the MVP award for the second straight season. He talked about how disappointed he was that there wasn't a World Series. He felt the White Sox had as good a chance as any team to get there. He also mentioned what had to happen for the White Sox to get another crack at it in 1995. "We've got to re-sign Julio Franco," he said. "He's the one player that's very key. It felt great getting those walks and standing at first base, knowing he can hit one in the gap."[5]

As things worked out, the White Sox never got

the chance to re-sign Franco. Because the baseball strike was still not settled in the spring, the entire 1995 season was a question mark, so both Franco and Darrin Jackson accepted offers to play baseball in Japan.

The strike came close to wiping out the entire 1995 season before the players decided to return to the field. When they reported to spring training, the White Sox had a different team. Top pitcher Jack McDowell had been traded to the New York Yankees in exchange for young prospects. Free agents Chris Sabo and Dave Martinez replaced Franco and Jackson. The White Sox not only were different, they weren't nearly as good as they were the year before.

Near the end of May, the White Sox traveled to Detroit for a weekend series with the first-place Tigers. It was supposed to be a showdown between Thomas and Tigers slugger Cecil Fielder, but before the series was over the starting lineup from both teams ended up in the record book. The White Sox and Tigers set a major-league record with 12 home runs in the Sox's 14–12 win. The Tigers opened up a 7–1 lead, only to have the White Sox fight back. Fielder hit two home runs, and Thomas hit one. It was clear that the White Sox still had a powerful lineup, but pitching remained a question.

Thomas is ready for anything at first base. His ability as a first baseman is often overshadowed by his hitting skills.

On June 2, with the White Sox in fourth place with a 11–20 record, White Sox general manager Ron Schueler fired manager Gene Lamont and replaced him with third base coach Terry Bevington. White Sox players felt responsible for Lamont's losing his job. "We've been under-achievers all year," Thomas said. "There's no blame to Gene, but the thing is not working, so somebody has to take the blame."[6]

Not much changed for the White Sox after they changed managers. The pitching was still terrible, and opposing teams weren't going to pitch to Thomas unless they had to. Thomas let his feelings known after he was walked three times in a loss to Toronto on June 7. "This . . . is getting old," he said. "It's chicken . . . baseball, and it's real boring. I'm sick of [it]. I can't stay focused, I can't stay aggressive. A long . . . year, that's what it's going to be."[7]

Said Toronto manager Cito Gaston, "Don't blame me for walking Thomas. Tell the White Sox to get someone to hit behind him."[8]

A weekend series with Cleveland at Comiskey Park in late June didn't have the drama that it was supposed to have when the season began. The Sox came in trailing the Indians by seventeen and a half games, and there was talk that the White Sox

In 1995, Thomas's ferocity as a hitter was catching up with him. Pitchers were intentionally walking him, and he was getting bored.

players were already giving up on the season. The Sox felt they proved otherwise by sweeping the three-game series, but it still left them fourteen and a half games out of first place.

"We've been so great the last few years, and people expect greatness," Thomas said. "We just swept a very tough team. This is a start for us."[9] Thomas backed his words with a two-homer game the next night, and the White Sox went on to put together a seven-game winning streak. The Sox moved into third place in the American League Central for the first time in the season.

They weren't able to gain on Cleveland, however. Despite a great early season by Indians first baseman Eddie Murray, Thomas was again chosen as the starting first baseman for the American League in the All-Star Game. He was the only White Sox player to make the team. Six Indians were selected.

Thanks to Thomas, the White Sox were able to beat the Indians at something. He slugged 8 home runs in the home run hitting contest the day before the All-Star Game at the Ballpark in Arlington, Texas. He edged Cleveland's Albert Belle to win the event for the second straight year.

"We are 17 1/2 games out at the break," Thomas said. "This brings some fun back into the

One area where Thomas has consistently led the American League is in bases on balls. He led the league in 1991, 1994, and 1995. In 1992, he tied Mickey Tettleton of the Detroit Tigers in the category.

game."[10] His fun continued the next night in the All-Star Game when he hit a two-run home run off Cincinnati's John Smiley. The National League went on to win the game, 3–2.

Although it was clear that the White Sox weren't going to win anything in 1995, Thomas kept hitting like a player chasing a championship. On September 13, he hit a pair of home runs in a 6–1 win over the California Angels. He also reached 100 RBIs for the season that night, making him only the fifth player in baseball history to drive in 100 runs in his first five seasons.

Thomas finished tied for second with 40 homers. Cleveland's Albert Belle led the major leagues with 50.

"I had a good year, but not as good a year as I am capable of having," Thomas said. "But if I can look back and say this was my worst year, I won't have anything to worry about."[11]

Thomas led the White Sox to second place finishes in 1996 and 1997. Both years he was selected to play in the All-Star Game but was forced to sit out because of injuries. During the 1997 season, Thomas batted .347 to lead the American league in hitting.

Chapter 8

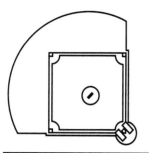

The Best Hitter

When discussion turns to the best hitters in the history of baseball, Ty Cobb, Ted Williams, Stan Musial, and Pete Rose are among the names that always come up. When the subject is the best power hitters of all time, another group of names are mentioned. Babe Ruth, Hank Aaron, and Willie Mays are the first three to come up.

Frank Thomas has the ability to be mentioned in both categories one day. Already, after just five full seasons in the major leagues, he is being compared to the very best hitters in the history of the game.

Ken "Hawk" Harrelson, the colorful announcer of the White Sox, is often asked about Thomas's talents as a hitter. More than once he has said, "Thirty years from now, if you take a poll of 100 hitters, they'll say Frank Thomas is the best hitter who ever lived."

Frank Thomas is considered by most fans to be the best hitter in major-league baseball today.

Many of the people who have been around baseball for a long time don't like to compare young players to the all-time greats for one reason: The all-time greats were successful for careers that lasted as many as twenty years. So the word "potential" is always used when discussing a promising young hitter.

Former White Sox hitting instructor Walt Hriniak has studied the hitting style of some of the best hitters of all time, including Ted Williams and Wade Boggs. Williams, the last player to hit .400 in a season (.406 in 1941), was able to combine a high batting average with great home run power. Williams hit 521 home runs in his career. Thomas has shown the same ability. Like Boggs, he has a gift for adjusting at the plate and making the most of nearly every at-bat.

It is easy to understand why Hriniak has enjoyed his time working with Thomas. "No one is perfect in this game," Hriniak said, "but of all the hitters in the American League, Frank is the best."[1]

There are a number of reasons why Thomas is a great hitter. His size and strength are a big advantage, because he can reach pitches thrown on the outside corner of the plate and still hit the ball hard. He also is blessed with a great eye at the

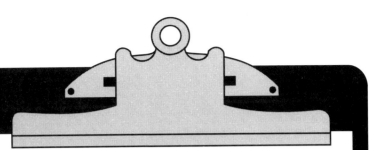

STATS

Top 10 All Time Career Batting Average Leaders

Player	Y	AB	H	Avg.
1. Ty Cobb	24	11,429	4,191	.367
2. Rogers Hornsby	23	8,137	2,930	.360
3. Joe Jackson	13	4,981	1,774	.356
4. Ed Delahanty	16	7,509	2,597	.346
5. Tris Speaker	22	10,197	3,514	.345
6. Ted Williams	19	7,706	2,654	.344
7. Billy Hamilton	14	6,284	2,163	.344
8. Willie Keeler	19	8,585	2,947	.343
9. Dan Brouthers	19	6,711	2,296	.342
10. Babe Ruth	22	8,399	2,873	.342

plate. He seldom swings at pitches out of the strike zone, which means that few pitchers are going to get him out on a bad pitch.

Most home run hitters strike out a lot and draw very few walks. Thomas is just the opposite. He is one of the hardest hitters to strike out and is one of only fifteen players in baseball history to drive in 100 runs and receive over 100 walks in a season. "That's what makes him a dangerous hitter," said Detroit Tigers slugger Cecil Fielder. "He doesn't want to come out of his strike zone and he doesn't. He'll stick with his guns until he gets a ball over the plate. And everyone has seen what he can do when he gets his pitch."[2]

Hriniak points out one other important thing about Thomas: He's not afraid to be great. Hriniak compares Thomas to the basketball player who likes to take the last shot in a tie game, or to the running back who wants the ball at the goal line. Thomas loves to hit with the game on the line.

Although he knows he was blessed with natural ability, Thomas is quick to remind everyone that it has taken a lot of hard work to become the player he is today. Many people are born with natural ability, but most never reach their potential because they fail to push themselves to be better.

The best players in baseball also get to the

ballpark early and leave late. They lift weights before the game. They take extra batting practice and fielding practice and ride an exercise bike to keep their legs strong.

Thomas has put in his time. "I followed my dreams," he said. "I worked hard enough to get it. A lot of people won't. Hey, nothing's easy for me. I did this myself."[3]

Visitors to the White Sox clubhouse will find an unusual message taped to Thomas's locker. It reads "DBTH," and stands for "Don't Believe the Hype." Thomas knows that a lot is going to be said and written about his talents. The message is there to remind himself that he has to keep working to reach his goals.

"When I'm on the field I'm very intense," Thomas said. "Every time I grab that bat, I'm looking for a hit. And if I don't get a hit I keep asking myself, 'Why did this guy get me out?' My teammates tell me, 'Frank, you're hitting .300, what are you worrying about?' They're beginning to understand me. I'm not crazy. I'm a competitor. I'm one of those guys who has to pour it on every night. If I get three hits, I'm disappointed if I don't get four."[4]

Being a star in a professional sport also means being a celebrity. Thomas likes the attention, and

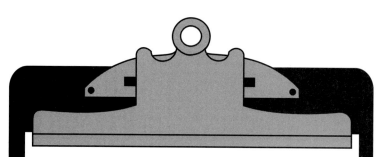

STATS

Of the players hitting in major-league baseball today, Frank Thomas is one of the best. Following is a list of the top ten active players (through 1997) with the best hitting records. Note: The list only includes players with at least 1,000 games played.

Player	AB	H	Avg.
1. Tony Gwynn	8,187	2,780	.340
2. Wade Boggs	8,453	2,800	.331
3. Frank Thomas	3,821	1,261	.330
4. Edgar Martinez	3,818	1,210	.317
5. Mark Grace	5,458	1,691	.310
6. Paul Molitor	10,333	3,178	.308
7. Jeff Bagwell	3,657	1,112	.304
8. Chuck Knoblauch	3,939	1,197	.304
9. Roberto Alomar	5,460	1,659	.304
10. Ken Griffey, Jr.	4,593	1,389	.302

the extra money he earns making commercials. He has started his own company, Big Hurt Enterprises, to deal with his off-the-field activities. Reebok named a shoe after Thomas. He also has deals with a trading card company and a bubble gum company.

Thomas doesn't spend all his time making money. He also set up the Frank Thomas Charitable Foundation to help people in need, especially children. He works with the Leukemia Society of America in hopes of finding a cure for the disease that killed his sister.

Frank Thomas and his wife, Elise, have two healthy children of their own, a son, Sterling, and a daughter, Sloan. They had their dream home built in a Chicago suburb and are happy to call Chicago their new home.

White Sox fans are happy to hear that. Thomas may never hit the ball farther than he did during that home run hitting contest in Pittsburgh in 1994, but he is sure to keep adding to the Best of Frank Thomas collection for years to come. Chicago sports fans have enjoyed watching Walter Payton perform on a football field and Michael Jordan do incredible things on the basketball court. Now they recognize the greatness of Frank Thomas on the baseball diamond.

Chicago fans have made Frank Thomas one of their favorite hometown players.

They're thankful that the White Sox recognized Thomas's abilities in time for the 1989 draft. Just as Bulls fans smile when remembering that two NBA teams passed on the chance to draft Jordan, they wonder how six teams could have missed their shot at the Big Hurt.

Thomas already has made those teams regret their decisions, but he promises that there is plenty of work still to be done. "I want to be one of those guys," said Thomas, "who makes people say, 'Some of the things he did, I don't think can ever be done again.'"[5]

Chapter Notes

Chapter 1

1. Alan Solomon, "All-Star Notes," *Chicago Tribune,* July 12, 1994, sec. 4, p. 8.

2. Alan Solomon, "Thomas Beyond Belief," *Chicago Tribune,* July 8, 1994, sec. 4, p. 1.

3. Alan Solomon, "LaValliere Injury Dims Thomas' Dazzling Night," *Chicago Tribune,* July 10, 1994, sec. 4, p. 3.

4. Alan Solomon, *Chicago Tribune,* July 8, 1994, sec. 4, p. 9.

Chapter 2

1. Skip Myslenski, "Perfectly, Frank," *Chicago Tribune,* August 7, 1994, sec. 4, p. 8.

2. Rick Reilly, "The Big Heart," *Sports Illustrated,* August 8, 1994, p. 19.

3. Myslenski, p. 8.

4. Reilly, p. 20.

5. Johnette Howard, "Frankly Speaking," *Sport,* April 1992, p. 43.

6. Myslenski, p. 8.

Chapter 3

1. Skip Myslenski, "Perfectly, Frank," *Chicago Tribune,* August 7, 1994, sec. 4, p. 8.

2. Johnette Howard, "Frankly Speaking," *Sport,* April 1992, p. 43.

3. Ibid.

4. Alan Solomon, "Thomas May Mean Powerful Sox Future," *Chicago Tribune,* March 15, 1990, sec. 4, p. 6.

5. Alan Solomon, "College Coach: Thomas the Best We've Ever Had," *Chicago Tribune,* November 11, 1993, sec. 4, p. 6.

6. Ibid.

Chapter 4

1. Paul Sullivan, "Thomas Having a Walk in the Park," *Chicago Tribune,* July 21, 1990, sec. 4, p. 6.

2. Alan Solomon, "Bad News for Sox' Foes: Thomas to Stay This Time," *Chicago Tribune,* March 18, 1991, sec. 3, p. 12.

3. Sullivan, p. 6.

4. Andrew Bagnato, "Sox Promote Thomas on a Big Moving Day," *Chicago Tribune,* August 3, 1990, sec. 4, p. 5.

5. Bob Logan, "Sox Turn to Thomas, Fernandez for Spark," *Daily Herald* (Arlington Heights, Ill.), August 3, 1990, sec. 3, p. 3.

6. Ibid.

7. Andrew Bagnato, "Thomas' Big Hit Helps Sox Bop Brewers," *Chicago Tribune,* August 4, 1990, sec. 4, p. 1.

8. Ibid.

Chapter 5

1. Mark Ruda, "Thomas' HR Sparks Sox' Win," *Daily Herald* (Arlington Heights, Ill.), April 23, 1991, sec. 3, p. 1.

2. Robert Markus, "Thomas Always Expected He'd Be a Hit," *Chicago Tribune,* August 30, 1991, sec. 4, p. 1.

3. Tim Sassone, "Bo to Play Monday vs. Royals," *Daily Herald* (Arlington Heights, Ill.), September 1, 1992, sec. 2, p. 5.

4. Tim Sassone, "Thomas, Fisk Lift Sox to 6–1 Victory," *Daily Herald* (Arlington Heights, Ill.), September 2, 1991, sec. 3, p. 7.

Chapter 6

1. Alan Solomon, "Sox's '2nd Chance' Rates No. 1 with MVP Voters," *Chicago Tribune,* November 11, 1993, sec. 2, p. 1.

2. Mark Ruda, "Thomas Garners Honors for August," *Daily Herald* (Arlington Heights, Ill.), September 3, 1993, sec. 3, p. 3.

3. Barry Rozner, "White Sox Shift Focus to Winning Next Season," *Daily Herald* (Arlington Heights, Ill.), October 13, 1993, sec. 2, p. 1.

4. Solomon, p. 1.

5. Ibid.

Chapter 7

1. Scot Gregor, "Thomas Proves He Can Never Be Counted Out at Plate: Big Hurt Is the Real Thing," *Daily Herald* (Arlington Heights, Ill.), April 2, 1994, sec. 1A, p. 15.

2. Scot Gregor, "Thomas Helps Sox Outslug Brewers," *Daily Herald* (Arlington Heights, Ill.), July 10, 1994, sec. 2, p. 1.

3. Ibid.

4. Paul Sullivan, "Players Scatter and Wait," *Chicago Tribune,* August 11, 1994, sec. 4, p. 1.

5. Mark Ruda, "Sox Need Franco for '95 Run, Thomas Says," *Daily Herald* (Arlington Heights, Ill.), October 27, 1994, sec. 2, p. 4.

6. Bill Jauss, "Sox Players Accept Blame," *Chicago Tribune,* June 3, 1995, sec. 3, p. 4.

7. Scot Gregor, "Thomas Starting to Show His Frustration," *Daily Herald* (Arlington Heights, Ill.), June 8, 1995, sec. 2, p. 1.

8. Dan Bickley, "Tired of Walks in the Park," *Chicago Sun-Times,* June 19, 1995, p. 75.

9. Paul Sullivan, "Sox Roll Over the Indians," *Chicago Tribune,* June 26, 1995, sec. 3, p. 7.

10. Scot Gregor, "Thomas Puts on Home Run Show," *Daily Herald* (Arlington Heights, Ill.), July 11, 1995, sec. 2, p. 1.

11. Toni Ginnetti, "Thomas, Sosa Each Did Their Share," *Chicago Sun-Times,* September 28, 1995, p. 96.

Chapter 8

1. Scot Gregor, "Thomas Can Never be Counted Out at Plate," *Daily Herald* (Arlington Heights, Ill.), April 2, 1994, sec. 1A, p. 14.

2. Ibid., p. 15.

3. Rick Reilly, "The Big Heart," *Sports Illustrated*, August 8, 1994, p. 19.

4. Jerome Holtzman, "Rarity Thomas Wins in a Walk," *Chicago Tribune,* August 16, 1991, sec. 4, p. 10.

5. Reilly, p. 20.

Career Statistics

Year	Team	G	AB	R	H	2B	3B	HR	RBI	AVG.	BB	SO	SB
1989	GC White Sox*	17	52	8	19	5	0	1	11	.365	10	24	4
	Sarasota*	55	188	27	52	9	1	4	30	.277	31	33	0
1990	Birmingham*	109	353	85	114	27	5	18	71	.323	112	74	7
	Chicago	60	191	39	63	11	3	7	31	.330	44	54	0
1991	Chicago	158	559	104	178	31	2	32	109	.318	138	112	1
1992	Chicago	160	573	108	185	46	2	24	115	.323	122	88	6
1993	Chicago	153	549	106	174	36	0	41	128	.317	112	54	4
1994	Chicago	113	399	106	141	34	1	38	101	.353	109	61	2
1995	Chicago	145	493	102	152	27	0	40	111	.308	136	74	3
1996	Chicago	141	527	110	184	26	0	40	134	.349	109	70	1
1997	Chicago	146	530	110	184	35	0	35	125	.347	109	69	1
Major League Totals		1,076	3,821	785	1,261	246	8	257	854	.330	879	582	18

*Minor Leagues

Where to Write Frank Thomas:

Mr. Frank Thomas
c/o Chicago White Sox
Comiskey Park
333 W. 35th Street
Chicago, IL 60616

On the Internet at:

http://www.majorleaguebaseball.com/bios/038703.sml
http://www.chisox.com

Index